M000009218

Cover designed by Rosanna Bub

Jean Bub
Visit my website at poemsbyjean.us

Printed in the United States of America

First Printing: Aug 2017

ISBN- 9781980846260

ROOTS OF THE RESILIENT

a collection of poetry and artwork

by Jean-Marie Bub

"I AM NOT LIKE OTHER PEOPLE.
I AM BURNING IN HELL
THE HELL OF MYSELF.

I DON'T HAVE TIME FOR THINGS
THAT HAVE NO SOUL."

— CHARLES BUKOWSKI

For my dad –

This is my letting go.
This is me forgiving, this is me opening my
arms to you
This is the growth and the change,
This is the understanding and the pain.

This is my resilience --
This is for you.

CONTENTS

intro to my ideology

There are days where volcanic eruptions take place
under my wrists, there are days where my scars
extend their exponential tissue, reaching upward as
if to come crawling to me for answers. There are
days when the desperation that's been living
beneath the surface of my skin begins to scratch at
the ceiling, begging for me to open up and let it out.
Before my suicide attempt, I probably would've

complied with its wishes, but it's been a while since I've last fed my skin a blade, and I refuse to let the lava pour out again. I have spent whole nights lying awake asking myself why I made it. That night, the devil came to me and said, "it takes less energy to exist, than to exist and burn out." The devil himself had told me to live -- from then on out I've looked at my attempt as some sort of twisted wake up call. I often think of the blood, and how upon feeling the sever of my vein, I also felt the will to live. You see, when you are mid-jump, just as you kick the chair from underneath you, after the blade has just grazed your skin - your life does not flash before you. The only thing that is rushing through your mind are the odds of someone finding you on time, and how your escape route was the wrong route to take. I often have flashbacks to the first time I opened my eyes again - barred windows and straps were the first thing I saw, and I have not been as pleased since. To have air in my lungs again was almost a fictional ideology; I had never thought I would see the light of day. I felt the throbbing of my arm but instead of emitting the same cruel energy that was directed toward me by many, I decided to shine light on my wounds. I remember the moment my gears turned again, the exact moment that everything began to make sense. This jagged terrain in which we call life is nothing more than a mere test administered to us by the universe, its purpose being to bring to light to who we truly are. It is a test to find ourselves. Upon making this discovery, I had promised myself that I would make up for the time I had lost in my battle with depression; I would set my heart free and finally become alive.

Why, you ask? Why did I do that to myself? Well, I could tell you about the time that two girls twisted my wrist, opening my cuts in the hallway at school – I can tell you about the time I had a pile of death threats waiting for me in my mailbox – I can tell you about the time I found out what alcoholism can really do to someone you love – I can tell you about the time that their words had kept me up at night, contemplating whether or not I was worthy of breathing the same oxygen as them –

or, I can let you read my soul.

I can let you dive into my mind and read the words I had wrote amidst the pain, the depression, the mutilation and the realization.

What they did no longer matters; this is *my* story, and I have vacated their hell long ago.

WARNING –

Some of my poems may contain material that can be
triggering to others. I have put asteriks (*) next to the titles of
works that speak about depression, self harm and/or abuse in
a graphic manner.

I have entered these pieces into my book in efforts to shine
light on mental illness, and to allow those who suffer to know
that they are not alone.

If you or someone you know is contemplating suicide,
engaging in self-harm or extremely depressive behavior,
please seek help as soon as possible. You are not alone in this
world. On page 89, I have listed multiple resources that will
allow you to seek help anonymously.
Always remember – this too shall pass.

DELIRIUM

* invalid invalidation of the soul

when you become a writer,
they either want to hear everything
or nothing
at all.

they'll stick their squalid hands inside your mouth
only to mutilate your tongue
with interrogation
accusation and pity,
they'll want to hear your story just
one
more
time, as if putting it on paper wasn't
a grueling sacrifice of the mind...

suddenly, every single detail
no longer belongs to you, no --
it becomes theirs
they claim your words as their own
they will take your suffering and brand themselves
with the very pain you were trying to
free yourself from
they'll remind you that you're okay this time,
that this time you made it out alive
you're okay, right?
what could possibly be wrong this time?
you wrote about it
it's over now
right?

they'll become sick of you
regurgitating the same old feelings,
they'll tell you
to write about something else --

as if you're in control of this beast
they'll even take a picture of your hurt
and make it their wallpaper on their phone --
remember when you wanted
to kill yourself?

remember those feelings?

remember all the blood
all the hate
the tears...
can you remember how intense you felt?

when you were gasping for air in the bathroom
and you could've sworn your lungs had collapsed
within your ribcage
and sank far down into your stomach?
can you remember that heaviness?
the heaviness that you woke up to
every morning
KNOWING
that you couldn't bear to set your feet on the ground
any longer
KNOWING
that you rather be floating
with the dust mites,
on a bookshelf probably --
can you remember the heaviness?

all of that
for it to be belittled into mediocrity?

when you
become a writer
all that you ever had felt will no longer be yours.
they'll take your words

they'll take your pain
they'll take everything
and leave you with nothing
nothing but a distant memory of how things used to
be...
before all of this.

* unbeknownst to myself,
I have shadowed my pain
from the world, in fear it'd
swallow me whole.

I have hid my scars,
mental and physical.
I have forced the dry and
uncoated pill of fear
down my throat,
casting a reign of silence
amongst myself, causing myself
to launch missiles of anger and retaliation
across the rivers that exist within my veins.

in my bone wages war, a war far too volatile
for the interference of man.
they tell me
I need to fight
the good fight,
but all that's come out of this destruction
has been a lingering numbness
that eats away at my surface,
causing dysphoria,
debilitation and desolation.

unbeknownst to myself,
I have cut the string
that was once attached to my heart,
in hopes it would detach me from
the destitution
I had fed to myself for ages.

I have ripped at the skin,
torn at the flesh,
in hopes of finding the truth that was buried

within me
so long ago; I cannot seem to find it.

unbeknownst to myself, there is a void that exists
far too deep
within the pores of my skin —
I had tried to reach for it once,
I almost didn't make it out alive.

- *living in hiding is no more liberating*
than taking a blade to your wrist

the lows

even though my heart is composed of twigs
that are constantly
being set aflame,
only to turn to ash again –

I continue to forage for small sticks
to repair the void that lies within.

I continuously attempt to hold onto my sanity,
to keep my shallow bones intact;
but I have worn thin.

my eyes are stained red and
it's not from the smoke
my body is in fluctuation between wanting to coat
my insides gold
and wanting to
light them on fire.

my brain lacks a simple chemical
that makes me feel like I'm drowning –
it's things like this
that make people feel like they have no home;
not even
within
themselves.

broken patience

I have asked for answers.
I have asked the universe,
and even to the man that exists in the sky, the one
that everyone talks so much about.
I have asked them

why you can't love me.

I have bled on my knees in church for you, Dad
I have called physicians,
I went running for answers.
none of them could point me in the right direction.
this may all be foolish, though;
this hoping for change,
this hoping --
as if you'd put down the bottle
as if you'd even bother to say my name
without spitting teeth out of your mouth.

I loved you, Dad
And I have tried to love you again.
but I can no longer check on you to make sure that
you're still breathing;
a person cannot live with holes drilled through their
heart
and I refuse to poke anymore
through mine.

you blindly manipulate yourself through life and I
refuse to be one of your pawns.
you have created more scars on my heart
than I've made myself, on my body –
it's time for me to move on now, dad
I have done my best
I gave all that I could give;

but I always seem to forget

you cannot squeeze blood
from stone.

you cannot ignore the pain
that has rooted you
into the same soil you've grown from.

it will find you,
it will make sure you don't forget —
it will sit in the back of your mind,
toying with your leaves,
itching at your branches.

and although you've moved on from the madness,
although you've awoken and began making your
bed again,
although you've washed the dishes
and cleaned the car
and watched your television
and arrived at your job at a timely fashion —

no amount of distraction
will ever be able to divert your attention
from the angst of your origin.

after all —
you carved its name
into your bark.

-   *suicide scars*

I've never gotten
the chance
to speak about
my abuse —

for every time I
opened my mouth,
there was always
a hand
waiting to be placed over it.

— threats of denial

healed but never forgotten

when your hand has covered her mouth for so long,
how do you expect her
not to speak?
how do you expect her
not to bite down?
how do you expect her
to not be afraid?

when your hand has gripped the flesh
and has bruised and broken through
how do you expect her
not to flinch?
how do you expect her
not to cry?

no woman wants to relive the past;
how do you expect her
not to be scared?
how do you expect her
not to question?

when your voice sounds so
much like her fathers
how can you expect her
to live life without fear
how can you expect her

to heal
or to
to love easily
to forget her hurt
to forget the past —

you are foolish if you think

her scars will heal
with time.

a pain like this,
an ache of this magnitude
cannot be hushed away,

you are mistaken if you think she'll
be quiet about this –
she wears her scars proudly, not because
you made them but because

she has survived –
and they will remain.

all hope, all pain

my eyes are dry,
as is my tongue
I'm tired of the bright lights
I'm sick of repeating myself –

I want to be free,
relinquished of this stale cage

I want release.

I no longer wish to confine myself
in this box

I want to feel alive,
I want to *feel alive.*

my father blooms in the spring —
you should see the way he tends to the flowers
I've never seen flowers
bloom like his,

I'm convinced he
speaks to them in his own
special language —
I wish I knew the words he spoke

in the winter,
my father goes dormant
his vibrancy fades,
his leaves
are no longer.

he wraps himself in,
he encloses himself within the
confinements of his basement,
as he speaks to himself secrets
only he knows,
only he's kept —

I wish I knew the words he spoke,
maybe then I'd know
what to say to him.

maybe then he'd know
what to say to me.

I wish he'd tell me.

                                        -    *untitled*

surrenderance

I've known from the beginning that this wouldn't be
easy,
this act of
giving myself to someone,
this act of
blooming in grace of someones holiness
someones kindness, even.

I have been trembling,
for I have hideous secrets
tucked away in parts of me
that no one has dare tried to explore, you see
I've taken the keys
and have bolted myself shut.
nobody has seen the entirety of my mind
nobody has demanded to see what's inside –

and I am terrified of the day
someone finds the key that I have hidden,

for I have these secrets
and for all this time,
they've only had
me.

you grip my wrists,
and I pull away,
fearing
that you'll notice my scars.

if you see them,
will you stay?

everybody else
has walked away.

façade of flowers

my father always made sure
he took care of our garden.
I remember the days he'd
spend outside,
under the hot sun. sweating –
but he never uttered a complaint.

the bushes would be cut to perfection,
from our front door
around the entire house, he'd
trim those bushes,
every week or so they'd grow back and
every week or so
he'd make sure they were proper once more.

our flowers would be in an infinite bloom.
the yellows and reds had never seemed to fade and
when they did, he'd replace or fix them.

he was good at that, fixing things
but he never seemed to pay as much attention to
the inside,

I had lived with mold my whole life and
his cigarette smoke vacated my lungs, I
never knew what it was like to breathe normally, I
thought this was normal.

there was dust and peeled paint, the
dishwasher broke and so two years later we
bought a new one but it's been
sitting in the middle of the kitchen for another four,

but my dad trimmed the bushes.
he was so fixated on those pesky little weeds and
the ivy growing between them,
that he never paid much attention to
what was going on inside, you see

there were holes in the walls and
I had no door,
the floor beneath my feet was breaking and
the walls surrounding me were screaming
and my room felt like it was caving and
everything was breaking,
even me –

everyone said we had a beautiful garden, and we did
but
nobody could tell
because of the flowers, because of those bushes
nobody knew
the hell that was brewing inside
nobody could hear
the cries for help, nobody heard anything
they just looked at the flowers –
and as the years

went on, my dad paid more attention to the yard,
maybe that says more about him
than it does about the way we
lived for so long,

now, even after I moved out
whenever I visit his house, he's
always outside

fixing the flowers.

pacing

I have been pacing
pacing between forgiveness
and actuality.

I have never favored the art of forgiveness.

from my hands drip the blood that you've spilt,
they're telling me to let it go.
how can I rid of these shards,
if they've been dug far too deep within my bones?

my mind is racing, back and forth determining
whether
I should tear the glass shards
you have so carefully constructed into my hands
or if I should soak them in the rose water you have
offered to me
that's been tainted in sin –

does forgiveness truly exonerate all the wrong that
has been dealt?
is that it?

I have been pacing.

double edged decisions

there are no absolutes.
there are no promises
there is no assurance –

only hope, only dreams.

and oh, how dreams fade over time
from being five and wild, hair in the wind
flowers in hand, mothers' heartbeat against your
ears –
you're told everything is within your reach
you are cradled, you are loved
you are holy.

and then there are no more flowers
its winter, and the wind has died.
your mother is far and
her days are numbered.
you are no longer holy, for sin is a pastime in which
you indulge

you have taken these promises
you have fed yourself this false assurance
and you have traded your dreams for a reality that
has been fabricated –

there are no absolutes.

you poured your salt into my eyes and
thank god
I blinked just in time to
avoid your grains of
lies, I

wondered if you'd ever
rain instead of hail but
I remembered —

monsters never change.

-   *blame*

brain fog

it seems as though with each
breath I take, I sacrifice
a sentence that pushes my passion
further into extinction –

it has become a normality,
this putrid defeat

with every waking moment
comes a blank;
an inevitable pause
that punctures through
my right hand

in which holds the pencil
to my tranquil creed,
my craft,
my livelihood,

my mess.

to be without...

it is hard to accept happiness
when all you've known is pain

when the epitome of your existence was nothing
more
than a double-edged sword,
filled with
restraint and doubts
no's and you can not's
and slippery grasps –
the abnormal
becomes your normal.

you notice the difference between you and others.
it's as if they're another breed of human,
a species foreign to you.
they speak with a different vocabulary –
they speak about happiness
as if it's within everyone's grasp
they speak about the sadness
as if it's an entity that can just be stripped from
one's soul.

however
they cannot begin to understand the wars you've
spent years fighting.

darling,
there is no need
to explain.

fuel

I am sick –
my heart is a chamber of manifested nightmares
only in my memory do I hold all
of the previous,
and plagued handshakes

my social encounters are merely just pathetic
facades
of forced normality.

I haven't wanted to dress myself
I haven't wanted to get out of bed
but something still pushes me

it shoves me over the edge that exists between my
conscious self
and my
devious thoughts
it plummets me to the bottom
only to show me that a
splattered body is nothing more than dead matter.

the universe takes ahold of me,
and thrusts me to the ground.
those who hold my heart close
have taken knives to my throat
and my chest is bound to explode –

I barely want to stay alive
but something keeps pushing me –
perhaps I should
wait around a bit
to find out
what lingers.

I am everyone's keeper
except for my own.

* a forward to my future lover

I'm sorry that I still finch when you touch me –
you see,
I haven't yet associated contact
with a positive connotation,
for I'm afraid that if I do –
history will repeat itself.

I'm still getting used to affection,
I don't mean to push you away –
my last "love"
didn't love me so gently
he left marks on my heart
and my hips.

I'm sorry I ask you to speak softly –
I can hear the booms of my father's voice
within the volume of your own –
it's not that you remind me of him, it's
just that yelling
is all I've ever known, and
I'd like to take some time away
from that state of mind.

I'm sorry I can't stand the way you chew, you see –
all of this sound
all of this *chaos* –
has caused an immense disturbance inside of me.

I might never be able to handle the rustling of paper
or overlapping, crowded voices.

just know that it's not your fault, my love;

it's theirs.

* we have created
this notion
that if the abuse cannot be seen;
it does not exist.

but, emotional abuse is just as valid
as the physical –
every time my father would blast two radios one tv
and his own voice
at 2 AM
I could feel the black and blues
forming within the grey matter
of my brain, and

even today, after I've moved on
and moved out,
I can't handle the static
I can't handle noise
I can't handle loud.

for every time I was denied exit of my room
and I was forced to be confined between these four
walls with no door, no privacy and no sanity;
I am filled with the cold rusted
nails of anxiety, I am terrified of
what lies outside, and
for every time I was told
I wasn't going to make it

or that
I wasn't nearly as good enough as they thought I
was going to be or that
I was pathetic or fat at 115 pounds or nobody will
love me with these problems of mine or that I was
good for nothing or a sorry ass or a child from hell –

it broke me.

I fear leaving my house alone
for I have this itch that comes up from within me,
telling me I'll never make it back.

I fear telling anyone about my childhood,
what memories are there to be found?
there was no Disneyland, no vacations, no pictures
only distant voices, no visits
and screaming in the kitchen.

I could never trust another soul,
for you have stripped me of everything –
you'd tell me you'd love me when I left for school
but when I came back, my journals were burned
and my clothes were stained with bleach.

my anxiety has interrupted my life
even after the hurt
even after it all –
I can never seem to catch my breath.

perhaps it's from the smoke you forced me to inhale
since I was 3,
perhaps it's just another panic attack from the
unexpected outburst that woke me at 6am.

you always told people you were a morning person,
but you never explained why,
or
in which way.

my mother tells me
my father cries about it now
that he
deeply regrets and realizes what he's done to me,

and I cry too.

for no amount of tears,
no amount of "sorry's"
and no amount of regret
will ever fix the damage that has been done.
I can never get my childhood back,
nothing can restore my innocence;

I cannot erase my scars,
and neither can he.

-   *you never hit me with your fists but*
        your words were enough.

distinct polarity

there is something you must understand –
we are not the same, we were
bred differently.

I was raised to survive,
I was raised to make the bread last –
on days I couldn't afford
school lunch,
I sat rumbling, booming;
exploding and tired
praying to get out of class, before
someone heard.

on days I
could no longer breathe and
I had no escape,
I'd find the closest vice,
I'd do whatever
it'd take to
numb the pain –

you see,
we weren't raised the same, I had no
outlet, I had no
bullet proof vest, I had no
warmth in the night, I hadn't a thought
about love –

all that was in my existence
was pain, and
all I wanted to do was break free,
you see,
we weren't raised the same --

I was raised to survive.
I was raised to get by,
to tough it out
to make it through –

we were bred differently, you and I;
I had no comfort.

I had to find comfort
within the walls
of myself

all while fighting the urge
to burn them
down.

objects in mirror may look closer than they appear

I lost myself,
I had masked my identity within *you,*
I had conformed to *your* idea of me –

I was not myself.

tiptoeing over my words
stumbling, tripping with every sentence,
in attempt to keep up
with someone who I was not.

you had made me believe that you loved me
and you had tricked me into loving someone
who was not yourself –
you were nothing more than
a mirage.

I had thought it was strange when you had me cut off
pieces of myself
to hold you together –

once I realized there was more missing of me
than there was of you,

I left.

there is no obligation with creations.
you see,
nobody asks to be born –
only you make that decision
when you decide to conceive,
so, don't tell me I must
hold my parents to any regard, I
refuse to hold them to any standard
but my own,
it's been engrained in our minds that we must
understand their fists, their words
their reasons,
their absence,
their seasons – it's been engrained in our minds
to accept the abuse, to just
take it then forget it, to hold this hurt within you, to let
it linger, to let it pry
to let it be the reason why we
stay the same, to let it be the reason why we
never change –

the only obligation
that exists with creation,
is for the creator.

it's to care.

                              –   *parental obligation*

* darkness & you

midnight has no modesty –
it does not knock lightly
on your front door, no –
midnight, in all its darkness,
kicks in the door
and ransacks your home,
it peels back your flesh
and lays its squalid
decaying
and frantic larvae of
melancholia within the pockets
of your body,
it crawls under your bedsheets
when you least expect it,

midnight gives no warning.
you can be sure that the sun will rise
but you never know when the darkness will leave.

midnight has no modesty,
but then again –
neither does
depression.

unstuck

I could transfer my
coagulated blood into this fountain pen
and tell you about those who have
chiseled away
at my sternum,

only making my heart
more vulnerable
only making it
more accessible
for you to toy and
play with, but
I'm tired and

it hurts
to speak about
the hurt.

I don't want to talk about
the sadness
anymore, it's like
guzzling down a shot of
glass shards, my throat
is sore and it can no longer
extend outward for you –
it hurts
to speak about the hurt.

in every vice
lies a trench —
do not think that just because
your drug of choice has been
rooted in the soil and
dried in the sun
that it's impermeable to the
ward of condemnation.

dependency
is dependency —
the denial of such detail
is nothing more than
a denial
rooted in addiction.

- *gluttony*

sometimes I wonder if my
bones were crafted from gun powder,
as I tend to explode
all too often.

it's difficult,
when you're a walking
ticking
time bomb.

it's especially difficult when
the people around you
are careless, reckless
and oblivious to your fragile condition,
even after you've
stuck a label on yourself,

"handle with care."

I venture through life as if
I'm not the one
in possession of the matches
the timer
the patience
the wires.

               –   *bipolar disorder*

different game, similar pain

to comprehend everything that
alcoholism is;
you must first pause --
contemplate,
and attempt to understand,
for it can never be
so simple.

but for the abused,
we seem to convince ourselves that
we don't have time to contemplate
or to examine this type of
hurt,
this…

thing
that we swear
is just so foreign to us –

we are so absorbed in our own hurt,
that we fail to see the wounded.

far too often,
we fail to realize
that their souls
are just as tormented
as ours.

no. 2

there's no section
in the card aisle for
"abusive dad's birthday."

combing through the cards
reading through the content,

I fall ill.

I'm sick of
this pretending,
this acting like nothing ever happened –

how can you not realize
the damage you've done
when I'm standing
right in front of you?

when I'm so obviously
bearing these scars?

am I
far too small
for you to see?

EUPHORIA

jean-marie bub

roots of the resilient

there will always be pain.
you will hold animosity in your heart
and it will hurt you.

do not be foolish enough
to let these times pass;

trees do not hide during storms.

they face torrential down pours,
they dig their root deeper into the soil --

you must do the same.

for years I have hid my scars
under my sleeves, unknowingly
malnourishing them
unknowingly
punishing myself --

but I can no longer conceal my pain,
or hide who I am.

as soon as I gave my scars to the sun,
they flourished.

> *-- there are sunflowers trapped*
> *beneath your sleeves:*
> *liberate them.*

to heal is to
reap revenge on yourself for all the times that you've
been coerced into basking in the glacial sun
of self-pity,

to heal is to
betray your illnesses and disorders, to
put down the blades and pick up the pen,

to heal is to
subdue and repress the lies you've been fed for
the entire duration of your life,

to heal is to
divulge your animosity,
to bathe in realization, and to diverge from
the torment —

to heal is to
feel alive again, to want
to feel alive again,

to heal is to
refuse agony.

to heal is to truly
become whole again — as you once were,
before all of this.

to heal is to
rid of all of the toxins that run throughout
your body,

to heal is to
do nothing
but bloom.

- resiliency

sometimes you need to
reroot yourself
back into the earth
in order to
find yourself again.

* *a triggered trigger warning*

I can still feel
the sharp corner of the blade
exiting my skin.
I still can feel the burning,
taking over my body
like a match kissing a pool of gasoline.

I can still feel the sensation of gratification arise
from within my lungs,
they clear as if I'm on a beach;
bliss.

it's been eight months since I've last parted my skin,
and my wrist is itching.
I can feel the fire raging underneath my arm
like a wildfire in a forest of redwood trees.

I sit here crouched over myself
dancing the blade between my fingers
slightly nipping at my fingers print —

is it worth it?
it's always worth it.
but is. it. worth. it.

I look at the scars that run down from my wrist to
elbow, as if I'm reading the receipt to my past —

I can remember ever tally I've ever etched
I remember the one that almost killed me
I remember which one I did with my friend in my
backyard,
under my tree.
I can remember the one that I did in school

and the one that happened for the very first time in the
shower;

I cannot
remember the way my arms used to look
before this.

I run my fingers down my wrist,
I close my eyes to read my story in braille;

it's not worth it.

the receipts I carry in the form of scars are enough
this is my proof
this is my pain
this is my permanent reminder;

it was worth it once before —
and that has to be enough
for now,
and for forever.

lesson learned

I know you miss my curves.
I know you miss the regions of my body that
no one else has seen.
see,
you had docked your boat on my private island,
my unexplored territory...
after seeing all of the bountiful resources I had
possessed,
after drinking from my fountain
of impermeability;
you tended to my gardens and took care of the
flowers
you made sure to keep everything just as you liked

but one day you decided to plant trees
that were far too foreign for my soil.

hesitantly, I accepted this.
consequently
you cut them down.

I was perfect for your relentless manipulation,
for I was untouched
I was pure
you had decided that I was yours.
you set fire to my foliage
you ravaged through my garden, uprooting my
flowers
killing most vibrant life.

I decided it was time for you to leave.

I know you miss my curves
you can probably still feel the indentation of my
waist
you probably still have a very vivid picture of what
my island used to look like,
before you attempted force me into submission.

I do remember your hands
and how they felt amongst the petals
and the leaves –

I know you miss my curves
but no part of me
will ever come close to missing your
poison;
never will I submit to a man
who tries to pin me down underneath his grip –

I rather burn slowly
and have all life devastated
than ever letting you graze my terrain,

again.

for April –

dry your eyes little solider
you will become bolder,
with bloody knuckles and untied shoelaces, you
shall persist

your heart may weight heavy,
but by the time you're seventy
you will find love and you'll find
your true paint.

dry your eyes little solider
broaden your shoulders,
with passion and an alarm clock you'll awake.

with your eyes hung low and your dreams to the floor,
you'll need more than your oar
to carry you up to the shore,
I assure you'll need your buckets
and your pain.

you smoke, and you cry,
you say life is but a lie
yet you sing, and you breathe.

you trudge up the stairs
not knowing if anyone is there,
you weep and you sing.

dry your eyes little solider
you're guaranteed to blossom bolder,
you were not cut from the same mold
as he.

you are strong, and your belt is buckled tight,

you have just the right might --
you are but a queen amongst the bees.

they envy your style and your diction.
although not fiction,
you are composed of conviction and of the trees.

they will try to bite you and redefine you
but little solider

you know better,
blow their minds and their hearts
until they cannot tell you how to part;
you are of your own distain.

little solider
you are bold, and you are booming
you are strong, on fire and you are moving
you are bright, and you have found
your paint.

for the wandering, anxious mind; an exercise

close your eyes
and imagine your frustration in the form of a ball
inside of your stomach
I want you to focus all of your energy on that ball
I want you to curse it
to yell at it
to condemn it to hell -- I want you to pour out
the gas and light a match.
I want you to focus all your energy onto
that damned ball,
tell it to go
fuck itself
throw it
step on it
disintegrate it.

I want you to cool it down
imagine it as an icy
blue mass
calmly bobbing within the contents of your
stomach.

take this delicacy
and hold it. feel it. examine it. which ball do you
prefer?
feel how your frustrations transformed into a cool
blue lake of
ripple and tide
feel
how you manifested that beast into nothing more
than a quiet, blue buoy.
focus your energy on that blue ball
I want you to put all of your love into this ball

I want you to watch it as it slowly transforms into a
bud
then into a red blossom
then into a rose.

I want you to remember
that your internal frustrations
are rooted by your personal manifestation.
I want you to remember
that no matter how hard it may get
or how hard it may be
you can always transform that anger
into a rose --

but first, you must change your focus.
then comes your energy.

jean-marie bub

my savior

my gift to you are my words.
when my throat collapses with avalanches of
anxiety
and my tongue becomes twisted in all its glory,
the pen is what saves me.

when I stutter like an overworked
car engine and
my hands shake as if they were experiencing
some sort of chaotic aftershock sparked by the
organ that lay behind my breastbone and slightly to
the left,

these sentences are all that can convey my meaning.

when my eyes wander, and I pick at my skin
instead of processing verbatim and
analyzing the language of your body,

my cursive on yellow college ruled paper
will form loops around your brain in efforts to reach
out to a place my voice couldn't venture.

words are my gift to you.
although my voice cracks and my tongue becomes
tied between my overriding thoughts and my
conscious breath,
I will always write down these words for you.
but despite having definition,

words can be as vacant as a man without a soul.
they can curl against tongues
without a single mispronunciation or error,
without meaning they are dense,
but words are my gift to you.
behind my vocabulary is weight.
the kind of weight that pulls on the strings
which link together the delicate cords
of your heart

a weight
that is a rarity.

allow me to bathe
in your impurities.
I want to absorb your
loathsome, I want your filth
to seep, deep
into the layers
of my skin, I want to know
how it feels, your pain—

allow me to shed you of
the dead skin
that encases you in sin,
I want to rid you of
the past that
lurks but never leaves.

allow me to cleanse
the most vile slivers
of your psyche, I want to
resurrect your soul and
banish your sloth

I'll only need you to
sacrifice your vice and bare
your scars.

if it makes you
more comfortable, perhaps I can
show you mine
first.

- *you are not alone*

I am rigid with strength,
I am as tough as the redwoods —
nothing about my structure
is soft.
I haven't been at war
with my mind
for all these years, just to
end up being subdued
into mere diminishment.

in this lifetime
I have already experienced
the pain
of several.

I have choked death
at my doorstep, not once
but twice —

I have been hardened
by this earth
and I will not revert back
to a spinelessness state —

I bear the scars
of my battles with pride
and I am not ashamed
to stand amongst the mountains.

I wish not to be soft
but to be
as I am —

rigid,
tough
and resilient.

- *façade of femininity*

much too often
my depression
becomes confused
with my lonesome —

but it is only within
my lonesome,
that I find solidarity –

and there,
I am whole.

when you cut off
the leaf
of a succulent plant,
and place it in water
and allow it time to heal
roots will begin to
extend outward
from its original tear.

in time,
and with care
it'll begin to sprout
into another plant, you see –

plants grow from the hurt
and so should we.

silence is my
cleared field, my
blossoming flowers, my
skin under the sun.
silence is my
peaceful abode,
my quiet library,
my home.

silence is my serenity.

I wish for nothing more than hush bliss,
my body yearns to be tranquilized
with the absence of sound —

the noise the loud the static the chaos
has caused a disturbance within me so great
that now, I have to find a way to cope
with the aftermath of its
earthquakes.

all of this noise has created
ripples in my stomach,
and I'm becoming seasick
waiting for silence
to become
immutable.

grow
with the pain.
do not let the pain
grow within
you.

cosmic lust

when we are decaying away in our casket,
being swallowed back up by the earth
lying in our box of compiled flesh and matter;
we are still us. you are stuck with yourself,
indefinitely.

it is time to caress your scars
it is time to get used to the cracks and curves
of your skin — this body is yours, this home,
this idiosyncratic molecular composition of love —
of you.

it is time to examine the raw contents of yourself,
for we have only one chance, before the earth
swallows us whole,
once more.

sheep, or speak

if yesterday you were silent
tomorrow you'll be silent too...

swallow every bit of pride
you have wedged
in the back of your throat,

spit up
your ego

let me hear your voice
allow me to partake in this journey
through your vessel –

let me hear your voice.

tell me –
what is
your truth?

while you're stuck
looking for love, the love
you should be looking for
is caving
inside of
your own
chest.

under/over whelmed

to feel everything so greatly is both a blessing and a

curse. my stomach does summersaults at the

thought of sharp objects and my skin curls up at the

smell of blood. when he tells me he loves me, my

heart swells to its maximum capacity – and all at

once, the universe stops… he loves me. my love for

him blossoms like flowers being engulfed by the

sun, except, in this instance, they never die. my

heart swells out of my chest at the thought of this –

bliss. but you cannot fool me -- my tongue hisses at

the slightest hint of negativity, my fists form into

nuclear weapons at the thought of disrespect… on

days when I can't get out of bed, and it feels as

though I have been drained of all my abilities – I

feel nothing. to be able to feel so numbly, is both a

gift and a curse. my chest remains unmoved when I

hear him say "I love you," my eyes close like steel

doors when I think about the chaos – when I'm

forced to school, my soul becomes separate from

my body and I can no longer comprehend what goes

through my head… my facial expressions decay,

my blood pressure dips like depressions on a

topographic map. oxygen runs through my hollow

veins, but the only thing I seem to feel, whether I'm manic or depressive, are my scars. they rooted themselves deep into my core, and show up on my skin like warning labels on solvents –

to be manic depressive, is both a gift and a curse.

nineteen minutes

We are there, alone - yet together. We breathe in a blissful synchronization, only fathomable in the rustling of the trees. It is quiet, the room is filled with only our breath and the hum of the air conditioner that lay below the bed. I can only seem to fall asleep next to him, if I'm to the left of him. I lay on the right, in observance. The room is cold, on this hot summer's morning - but he serves as my warmth. I watch him. His arm is draped across my shoulders, he is turned into me, his heavy legs intertwined with mine. He is asleep. It is 9:47 AM. I study the birthmarks that the Angels had left upon his cheeks, just below his eyes. He is peaceful. I quietly crack my knuckles, his foot twitches. His phone dings. Nothing breaks my attention with his face. His aura is that of a divinity that derives from the soil, he is the Earth's son - perhaps he could be the moon, quiet and cool to the touch. His heart gives him away, he is raging of fire and burning with vigor. I smile a bit and leave a kiss upon his left cheek. He snores, I giggle. His olive skin sends chills down my spine, I flashback to a time when we lay upon the beach, mid-November, watching the waves creep up to the shore, the lights of a bridge in the distance. His skin was tougher then and we weren't so sure but his hands still sent shivers along the surface of my skin. I have never been so infatuated with another human before. He smells of a mixture of his cologne and sweat. His natural oils cascade down his face like rain during a sun shower, he is glowing. His snores become monstrous now, but his lungs remain quiet. He is booming with a sound so deep that he wakes himself up. He pulls me in tighter, I drop my phone. I can feel his heart beat now, against my back. I slowly get up, removing the green sheets that were sheltering us from the cold, and move to the left side of the bed. My feet cry and as I walk upon the freezing hardwood floor, carefully navigating through the wires and cold wood. I crawl back into bed, and my feet touch his, jolting him awake. He looks at me with his fire brown eyes, an eyelash falls onto his cheek. I go back to a time when he wrote my name down for a poetry slam, where I first shared my words out loud, where I cried in the car after. I remember my heart beating fast and his soothing voice slowly calming me down, I remember writing about it later that night comparing him to the moon caressing its tides. I remember that night with every emotion I felt, I kiss him. He doesn't know that I'm thanking him, but I do it anyway. He watches me. With every blink signals an "I love you," with every breath motions me to come closer. Every expression he forms transports me back to a time just like this - in another place, another time, another reality. I hold his warm face between the tenderness of my palms, I kiss his brown, pink bottom lip with the thunder he bestowed in me. His lips remind me of car rides, how I would kiss his lips whenever he came to a stop, how I would admire his portrait underneath the red traffic lights. His lips remind me of his left turns, his eyes remind me of what made me decide to pick up the pen again. He wraps me in his arms, I slide my phone under the pillow. My eyes start to water, my vision clouds. 10:06 AM. His heartbeat is next to my ear, and I fall asleep to the song I was born to hear,

we are sure.

ON
FLUIDITY &
THOUGHT

<u>observation</u>

to be alive is more than just to breathe. it's to feel, to do, to wonder, to wander. it's to ponder. to count the number of freckles on your lover's face, to travel to a place of serenity to find your peace of mind. it's more than this. it's more than the selfies, the subtweets, the depression, the system. a large majority of the things around us are merely just a social construct. some scientists consider math to be the only viable and reliable reality that there is, but you are all stuck in trivial things that we've conjured up within the past couple of years; the trends, your parent's money, the amount of likes you received on your most recent post -- you see, you've become stuck. you lost yourself in the value of other people and their objects -- but it doesn't have to be that way. ponder, wonder and wander. what they think about you is not important -- what you have inside of you, what you have constructed and developed within your genes is what matters. but even then, you don't have to make it matter. you have the power to adapt, to change, to thrive.

copycat
I remember how you reacted
when I first laid my emotions
onto paper;
I was a bitch
I was a mess
I was all too much for you --

you ripped me to shreds,
invalidated my pain
prayed for my failure
burned my book --
yet still followed my story.

and now, all of you
lay your fakeness down and print your initials
at the end of your plagiarized,
poorly written stanzas
as if it was your idea

as if you knew what it meant to
CONVEY feelings
as if you knew what it meant to be
AUTHENTIC...

revert back to your natural state.
there is no room

for poison-dipped

tongues.

most of the time,
women who believe that
they *need* a man
to survive --
become trapped beneath their feet.

you have yourself –
that is enough,

we are of stardust and glory;
from our womb grows life,
from our hands grow vines of fortitude,
if anyone can survive on their own –
it's us.

-   <u>lies our mothers told us</u>

<u>on the universe and it's pain</u>

in a world filled with an indescribable amount of pain, hatred and grief — I think it's wise to humble yourself amongst your tribulations, whether they're pinching at or charring your flesh. no pain is greater than or weaker than another — no matter it's form, internal and/or external, no pain is equal in its ability to be visible nor in its ability to fluctuate and impact. however, all pain is wicked. I cannot see the lies you hold within your chest, nor can you see the ones I hold in mine. we all seem to subconsciously hold these illustrious visions of grandeur, as if there is no return. as if there is no consequence for such thought. your pain cannot compare to mine, for there is no competition within the universe's premise of hurt. I think it's wise to speak your pain into the universe — to use your voice as a vessel, so that it will acknowledge that pain. your grave return will be reaping what you deserved to have sowed. no matter your destitution, or your destitutions form, no matter how harsh or subtle, we all inconsequently chose how we'd like to utilize this pain that's been bestowed onto us. you can choose to let to let your pain liberate your soul, let it be your excuse or wait around for divine intervention — but I much rather say I liberated myself — there is no point in waiting aimlessly for a sign. This is your sign. You are your own sign — be your own vessel. Humble yourself. Articulate your words wisely. Remember — the universe is watching.

<u>you, a mockery</u>

I do not create simple things
for I fear the attraction
of a simple mind --

how sad is it to only be able
to produce close to nothing
with no intention
no meaning
no purpose --

I do not like simplicity,
for life is not simple;
we are a beautiful symphony of chaos --
either on the brink of total collapse
or complete
and utter eminence.
how sad is it to live amongst all of that turmoil,
and only being able to piece together letters
to form words,
and not an endearment of your soul onto paper.

to be a writer
is more than having the ability to throw your words
into the universe.

to be a writer is to be unapologetically real,
unapologetically raw --
to live the truth
to be the truth

to spread the truth.

petty distraction

a lot of the time, we lose sight on what's important in life — we tend to focus on the trivial, material things; what people are saying, what I'm going to wear, but mostly if others are going to like you. it takes a while to break this thought process, most of us lose it by the time we're out of high school or college — but if insecurities have eaten you alive for the majority of your life, if anxiety plagues your mind at every waking moment, it'll be a harder mentality to shed. you'll still walk around debating whether or not the cashier heard you stutter and you'll still be self-conscious of the way your hips look in jeans. when your conscious has been beaten up and manipulated by others for most of your life, it's hard to let all of that pent-up pain go. it's hard to have the confidence to be unapologetically you — but we must take baby steps. you must slowly piece yourself together like the grand mosaic that you are. you must slowly caress your hips and love them in skirts or with nothing on at all. you have to see past the words, the hurt, the abuse and begin to see your very own silver lining. it's out there, and it's waiting for you.

you just have to be willing to see it.

loss of innocence
from the very beginning,
they tell us we can conquer the world.
so, we try -- oh, we try...
we want to take over the earth
replenish all that has been devastated
restore all that has been lost.
we see the triumph as nothing but righteousness
so, we continue with our chests,
filled with justice and desire
we march forward.

but then they tell us we can't.
they tell us
over and over
that this "righteousness" is an unachievable feat -

but we try until it hurts.
we dirty our nails with the blood that we've shed
for this dream
this dream that they've fed us for our entirety
we cannot let go,
we say, until we do.

there comes a point in this life
where we let go we seemingly
all forget at once –

in unison, we forget.

what happened to the triumph
where have we forgotten
our vigor?

enigma

I am afraid of reality and the ocean. my hands tremble and I haven't door. my chest caves when I hear the word "dad" and I enjoy breaking glass; my eyebrows are kept neat and my wrists are scarred. I can remember to water my plants, but I can't remember where I'm going; I can't understand the concept of home and I have lost the keys to my house. my dog only shows me affection when I have to leave, and all of my red pens have become lost; I was told that I am an enigma. I lost three of the buttons that were once attached to my shirt and I am looking at apartments; I haven't done my homework and my shoes are untied but my yellow scarf keeps me safe. beer tastes like contradiction and my mom told me all I do is destroy but the leaves of my plants are green and bountiful; my lips are red and nobody will understand the growing pains I had to endure at 8 and 12 and 15 but the ozone layer is thinning; I am 17 years of age and life feels like a gigantic organ with holes and my hands don't feel real.

I am afraid of reality and the ocean;
if nothing makes sense
then neither will I.

compound of adoration

much like atoms packed within a solid, we vibrate at the same frequency as we lay upon each other. your goosebumps fit within the crevasses of my own as your sweat pools into the abyss of my collarbones, and although there is no music, your body flows along with mine. we move rhythmically amongst the waves that exist upon your smooth sheets, our composure being held with the fluidity of water — your words pour out onto my skin, and you are alive. the minute pressure of your exhalation lingers on the surface of my epidermis, I tremble. I am alive. from your hands drip gold; a pure substance which is derived from the chambers of your heart, from the center of all purity, from the center of the earth. on the days we are far from home, I can feel the tendons of my heart stretching out like arms, in efforts to find you again. it reminds me of your every swift movement, every soft word that's ever raced across your lips and I quiver at your opulence and marvel at the sound of your breath upon my skin. our vibrations send shockwaves to foreign lands, we find comfort in the warmth we create within one another... much like the atoms that come together to make up the matter that exists in this world, we form as one. you are my core.

june second

june 2nd. this day has always felt immense to me, but today I forgot. I let it slip through the cracks of my mind, as if it was sand of some sort — it's the first year I've ever forgotten what happened to me on this day. it was only until I wrote down the date during work that it struck me — it's been six years since I tried to kill myself. it's been six years since I allowed my pain to engulf me in darkness. it's been six years. six. years. it feels as though it was yesterday that I was crouched over on the floor, dry-heaving, bleeding, mind immersed in torment, hand gripping blade. it feels as though it was last week since I was in the hospital — I can still see the barred windows that embroidered my white painted room. the steel doors were so heavy when they closed, which, they rarely did, but I can still hear them in every door that shuts. I haven't broken the habit of jumping when I hear loud noises. it feels as though my wounds are still fresh — perhaps that's because they are, although my wrists have scarred over I can still feel them bleeding inside of me, blood tends to find its way into the voids that exist within my body. not a day passes that I don't think about this hurt, this agony.

I write so much about it because this is all I know —
and even though I've seen "the light," it will never been
enough to erase the scars that exist within the grey
matter of my brain. some might describe how I feel as
wallowing, some might say that it's time for me to
move on, but this is my resilience. this is how I've
chosen to recover — I cannot trick my mind into
thinking that it's happy. no amount of affirmations or
prayers or hugs or well wishes will make me feel okay.
the only thing that'll ever bring me close to feeling
whole again is the act of dispelling this pain onto paper.
so make fun of me if you wish, make fun of my healing,
go ahead — you will be no different than those who
drove me to carve highways on my wrists; if my suicide
attempt wasn't taken lightly, why should my recovery?
why should I be shunned for being so open about
happened to me? who brought shame to the expulsion
of pain? I'm human. these things happen — why do
you want to pretend like they don't? is it because it
makes you more comfortable? writing makes me
comfortable. I am still human. I still bruise. I still have
flashbacks of that night, and many others. I have to live
with these scars, I struggle — I relapsed this week. I
have flesh. I have to live with these memories — so

please. do not judge me. I'm recovering. although I might seem strong, I am still weak. my roots have just begun to dig deeper within the soil, and it's been six years. I know I help many of you, but make no mistake — I still ache. I still have triggers. I need help, too. my progress is slow, but my hope is strong. it's June 2nd. it's been six years, but the knife that's been placed between the disks of my spine hasn't dulled a bit. it still hurts. but it's been six years, and I've begun to bloom.

**for those that've taken their lives
due to the monsters in their minds:
a message from someone who's tried.**

I'm sorry they didn't notice. I'm sorry they didn't ask
you about your day — when you're plummeting at
what feels like over 100 miles per hour, a simple "how
are you?" can sometimes be the only amount of friction
you need to slow you down from hitting the bottom.
I'm sorry if they might've ignored you, or spoke over
you when you attempted to speak. I know how loud
everything feels when there's nothing but numbness
circling inside of your head. I know what you were
trying to say when you exposed your scars by wearing
short sleeves to work for the first time yesterday, I'm
sorry they failed to answer your cry for help. I'm sorry
if they invalidated your pain. the darkness swallowed
you, and that should've been enough — but you are not
culpable for their ignorance. I'm sorry they didn't
notice you were crying in class, although you sniffled
loud enough for them to hear. I know sometimes it feels
like they twisted the knife that's been lodged into your
heart even deeper. I know that sometimes it hurts so
bad you go mute. I know how hard it is to speak about
what lurks in your mind, but my love, you never over
exaggerated. you remained righteous for every way you
expressed the thoughts you had trapped within you. I'm
sorry they didn't pick up the phone when you were
contemplating picking up the blade. I know you told
yourself that it was just because that you weren't good
enough for them; but they were inconsiderate. I'm sorry
all of the signs went ignored. I'm sorry you became a
statistic. I'm sorry they thought you were the strong one
and assumed you'd remain resilient throughout your

battles. I'm sorry you spent your life helping everyone but yourself. I'm sorry you were in so much agony that you not only took your own life, but were tormented for weeks, months, and years living inside a body that did not want to heal itself. I'm sorry you were alone.

nothing I can say will bring you back, I know this. I wish you were here, so I could've told you this —

I know it seems that all has lost its luster — but that doesn't mean you have, too. I know the demons whisper agonizing sweet nothings in your ear when night falls, they did to me as well — over time I started to believe the words they tormented me with, and I gripped the blade. when I tried to take my own life I was blinded with ignorance. I was convinced that suicide would fill the void, cure the pain, end the war in my veins. upon waking up, nothing went as originally planned. I can still remember the first breath of air that was administered to my lungs. it felt like liberation. it was a new beginning. you see, severance was never the answer. I needed a wakeup call. I needed someone to help. I needed to find myself. you belonged here, with the flowers and the trees. this earth belonged to you as much as it does to them.

I'm sorry you didn't live to see this.

you deserved happiness, and you deserved our help.

but most importantly, you deserved our compassion.

I am so sorry.

If you or someone you know needs help, advice or just another person to speak to, please, *do not hesitate* to call the numbers listed below. There are people in this world that care about you, and are willing to help you. Please reach out. It's never too late.

RESOURCES (IN THE US)

ADDICTION

Drug & Alcohol Treatment Hotline
800-662-HELP

Ecstasy Addiction
1-800-468-6933

Cocaine Help Line
1-800-COCAINE (1-800-262-2463)

ANXIETY

Panic Disorder Information Hotline
800- 64-PANIC

Anxiety Helpline
1-888-826-9438

DOMESTIC VIOLENCE / CHILD ABUSE

Domestic Violence Hotline
800-799-7233

Domestic Violence Hotline/Child Abuse
1-800-4-A-CHILD (800 422 4453)

Child Abuse Hotline
800-4-A-CHILD

Family Violence Prevention Center
1-800-313-1310

Missing & Exploited Children Hotline
1-800-843-5678

Healing Woman Foundation (Abuse)
1-800-477-4111

Incest Awareness Foundation
1-888 -547-3222

Runaway Hotline
800-621-4000

Victim Center
1-800-FYI-CALL (1-800-394-2255)

EATING DISORDER

Bulimia and Self-Help Hotline
1-314-588-1683

National Eating Disorder Association
Information and Referral HelpLine
1-800-931-2237

National Association of Anorexia Nervosa and
Associated Disorders (ANAD)
630-577-1330

Overeater's Anonymous
1-505-891-4320

FINDING SUPPORT / RESOURCES

Help Finding a Therapist
1-800-THERAPIST (1-800-843-7274)

National Alliance on Mental Illness (NAMI)
1-800-950-NAMI (6264)

LGBTQ+

Gay & Lesbian National Hotline
1-888-THE-GLNH (1-888-843-4564)

Gay & Lesbian Trevor HelpLine
Suicide Prevention
1-800-850-8078

PREGNANCY / ABORTION

Post Abortion Trauma
1-800-593-2273

OptionLine
1-800-712-4357

American Pregnancy Helpline
1-866-942-6466

Teenline
1-800-852-8336

Maternal Assistance Program
713-680-TEEN

RAPE / SEXUAL ASSAULT

Rape (People Against Rape)
1-800-877-7252

Rape, Abuse, Incest, National Network (RAINN)
1-800-656-HOPE (1-800-656-4673)

Sexual Assault Hotline
1-800-656-4673

Sexual Abuse – Stop It Now!
1-888-PREVENT

Victim Center
1-800-FYI-CALL (1-800-394-2255)

SELF HARM

Self-Injury (Information only)
(NOT a crisis line. Info and referrals only)
1-800-DONT CUT (1-800-366-8288)

SUICIDE / CRISIS LINES

Adolescent Suicide Hotline
800-621-4000

Adolescent Crisis Intervention & Counseling Nineline
1-800-999-9999

Suicide Prevention Lifeline
1-800-273-TALK

Suicide & Crisis Hotline
1-800-999-9999

Suicide Prevention – The Trevor HelpLine
(Specializing in gay and lesbian youth suicide prevention).
1-800-850-8078

IMAlive -online crisis chat

Teen Helpline
1-800-400-0900

Youth Crisis Hotline
800-HIT-HOME

INTERNATIONAL SUICIDE HOTLINES

Argentina: +5402234930430

Australia: 131114

Austria: 017133374

Belgium: 106

Bosnia & Herzegovina: 080 05 03 05

Botswana: 3911270

Brazil: 212339191

Canada: 5147234000 (Montreal); 18662773553 (outside Montreal)

Croatia: 014833888

Denmark: +4570201201

Egypt: 7621602

Finland: 010 195 202

France: 0145394000

Germany: 08001810771

Holland: 09000767

Hong Kong: +852 2382 0000

Hungary: 116123

India: 8888817666

Ireland: +4408457909090

Italy: 800860022

Japan: +810352869090

Mexico: 5255102550

New Zealand: 045861048

Norway: +4781533300

Philippines: 028969191

Poland: 5270000

Russia: 0078202577577

Spain: 914590050

South Africa: 0514445691

Sweden: 46317112400

Switzerland: 143

United Kingdom: 08457909090

USA: 18002738255

jean-marie bub

ACKNOWLEDGEMENTS

I'd like to thank Dennis, my love, for always supporting my endeavors, and for truly loving me unconditionally. My next book is for you.

I'd also like to thank Tatum. Thank you for all of the support you've given me within the last three years. You are the absolute bestest friend a girl could ask for. Thank you.

Most importantly, I'd like to thank my mother, Rosanna, for not only illustrating the cover of this book, but for truly showing me what it really is to be strong – thank you for raising me in such a way that I'd end up becoming so resilient. Thank you for sharing your pain with me, for never holding back – thank you for all that you've done. I love you abundantly.

ABOUT THE AUTHOR

jean-marie bub lives on long island, in new york.
she is an avid lover of art, science and all things that
contain passion and
emit love.

roots of the resilient is
her second self-
published book. her
poems reflect her life
and experiences she has
been through. she hopes
to give a voice to those
who cannot speak.

her work has been featured in national anthologies,
barnes and nobles, and her book, "pulchritude and
soul," has also been introduced into her high school's
health curriculum, to bring awareness to the importance
of mental health, as well as the addiction that self-harm
really is.

Made in the USA
Middletown, DE
21 July 2018